The Park

Marilyn Woolley

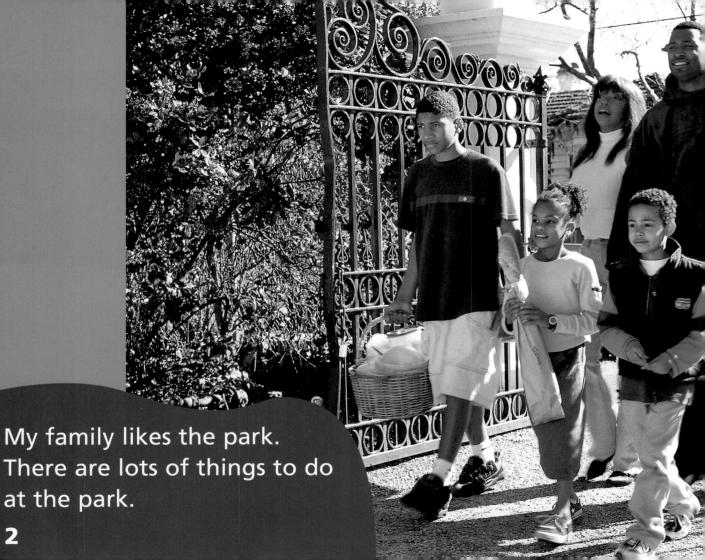

My family likes the park.
There are lots of things to do
at the park.

2

Look at the things to do on this map.

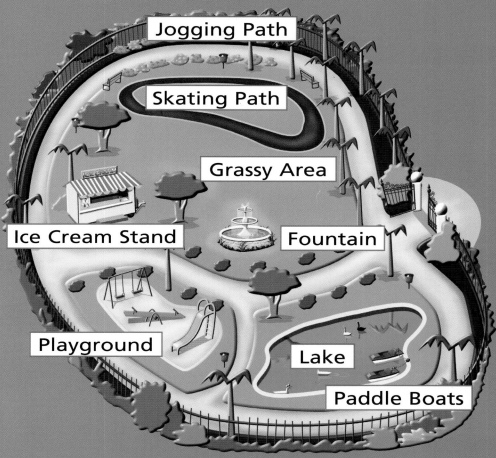

Jogging Path

Skating Path

Grassy Area

Ice Cream Stand

Fountain

Playground

Lake

Paddle Boats

3

I like the playground at the park.
I like the slide and seesaws.
I like the swings, too.

4

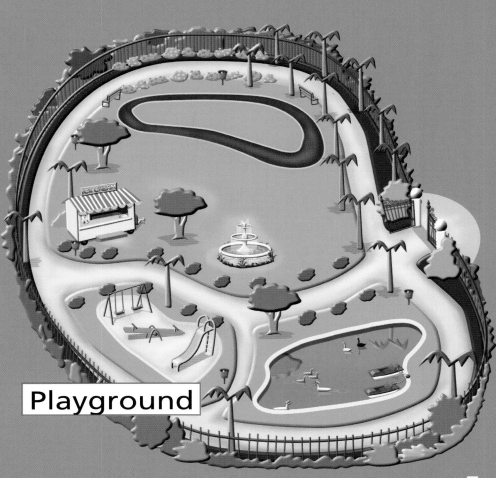

Playground

My brother likes to skate
at the park.
He skates on the skating path.
He skates around and around.

6

Skating Path

My mom likes to fly a kite at the park.
I like to fly a kite, too.
We fly our kite in the grassy area.

8

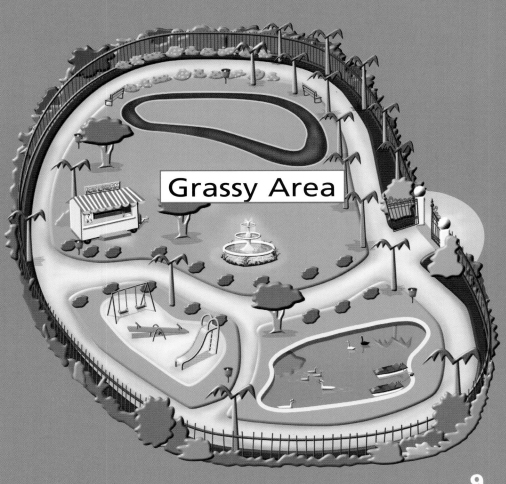

Grassy Area

My dad likes to jog at the park.
He jogs on the jogging path in the park.
My dad likes to keep fit.

Jogging Path

My sister likes the ducks on the lake.
My mom likes them, too.
They feed bread to the ducks.

Lake

My family likes to have a picnic in the park.
We sit on the grass to have a picnic.

Grassy Area

What else can you do at the park?

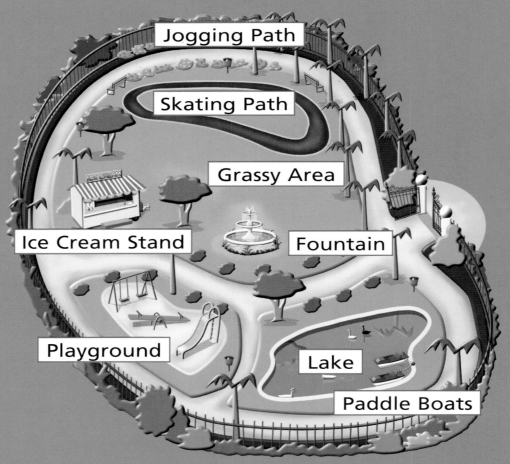

Jogging Path

Skating Path

Grassy Area

Ice Cream Stand

Fountain

Playground

Lake

Paddle Boats